Landmarks

A Haibun Collection

Landmarks

A Haibun Collection

Ray Rasmussen

Haibun Bookshelf Publishing

Edmonton, Canada 2015

Published by Haibun Bookshelf Publishing

Website: http://raysweb.net/hbp

Address: Edmonton, Alberta, Canada

Designed and typeset by the Author

Cover & Inuksuk Images by the Author

Fonts: Josefin Sans & Zest Medium

Softwares: MS Word, Adobe Acrobat Pro, Createspace

ISBN: 978-0-9948138-0-0

Printed in the United States of America

10 9 8 7 6 5 4 3 2 1

Dedications

There is no end of things in the heart
~ Li Po, Tr. by Ezra Pound

For:

Nancy, Teal & Terra

Mary & John
who kept our family connected &
helped our parents enjoy their last years

Sandra

mother of my children

Frances

poet mom

The Road goes ever on and on
Down from the door where it began.
Now far ahead the Road has gone,
And I must follow, if I can,
Pursuing it with eager feet,
Until it joins some larger way
Where many paths and errands meet.
And whither then? I cannot say.

~ J.R.R. Tolkien, The Fellowship of the Ring

Contents

Introduction

The cover image is of an inuksuk - a stone cairn in human shape. Inuksuit[1] in various sizes and shapes are used as landmarks as the peoples of the Arctic region travel from place to place in a somewhat featureless landscape.

I live in southern Canada where inuksuit can be seen in front of homes, in parks and along roadsides, which indicates their widespread appeal. The cover shows one that resides near a cottage where I spend time canoeing, walking, putting up winter's wood supply and writing.

This collection represents my 15-year journey wandering about in a poetry place called "haibun." Each took between a few months to a year to write, revise, receive an editor's blessing and finally appear in a journal. Thus each is a personal landmark in my writing practice.

The subjects are based on memories of childhood and school and more recent experiences related to wilderness journeys, later-in-life romance, retirement, teaching, aging and philosophical musings. The collection jumps from subject to subject, akin to the rather random order in which I remembered or lived them.

~ Ray Rasmussen

1. Inuksuk is singular, inuksuit plural. It is variously spelled inukhuk, inussuk, inukshuk in different Artic region languages.

Section 1: Haibun

Warmth

I miss them, my daughters when they were young.
Reading *The Hobbit* in winter, snuggled in close,
bodies and fire keeping us warm, rewarded with
their pleas: *Just one more page, please dad!
Please!*

I don't remember being read to, but when I was
sick, my mother sang lullabies while tucking me
deep under the covers, only my nose and ears
sticking out.

I remember the smell of camphor, the melodies,
but not the words.

old friends –
I place more wood
on the campfire

All That Remains

The email is from college friends with whom I've not had contact for 30 years. They write:

> For some reason that we cannot entirely explain we decided to try and find you. We were just at lunch with friends, some of whom are quite a bit younger, and we found ourselves telling them about the 60's we shared at the University of California, the anti-war marches, the sit-ins, the Fillmore concerts, Joan Baez singing "We Shall Overcome," the hippies and drug scene. So here we are contacting you.

What to say? Marriage and children. Affairs and divorce. Friends and enemies. Work and retirement. Successes and failures. Too many regrets.

And why say anything beyond how difficult the telling is?

> winter snow –
> peony roots somewhere
> beneath the crust

Folding Knife

Spring Equinox. My tent is pitched near the ruins of a cliff dwelling. When I left for the Southwest, she gave me a folding knife and said, "This is so you think of me when you do your man's thing." The wooden handle is a polished burl with swirls like those in the striated sandstone walls.

I use the blade to poke through the dirt, isolating flakes of chert – the hard stone the Anasazi used to make arrow points. They too once sat here doing their men's thing, sharpening stone with stone in preparation for the hunt.

In the moments before darkness, there's a rustle in the willows. I imagine it's the hunters whispering about the women they left behind, whispering so as not to startle the deer below.

The fire gone to embers, I fold blade into handle, body into sleeping bag, mind into pre-sleep wanderings, remembering the time she slipped from our bed, walked nude with a woman's willow-sway, all curves, and reached out to close the lace curtains, remembering the feel of holding her close, the feel of her graceful hands raising a fire in my body.

full moon rising –
coyotes yip their way
into the hunt

The Bathrobe

One rack in the men's shop contains richly colored robes with fancy lapels, threads that James Bond might wear while romancing one of his many women. I reach for bold red and gold plaid with shiny black lapels.

Suddenly awake, anxious, I glance at the hook on which my robe hangs. Relief! Still there.

There are large patches where I've had my tailor salvage it after large holes grew in the wrong places.

"They're not that expensive. Why not just buy a new one?" the tailor, a very practical woman, had suggested.

"No," I had said, "I like this robe."

"Do you want exactly the same kind and color of cloth?"

"It's just a robe. Do your best."

Having had it patched didn't relieve my fears. When my wife looks at it, I see the rag basket in her eyes. When it falls to the floor, the dog happily sleeps on it.

Men reading this know that the robe and I won't soon be parted. It's comfortable and my life isn't a Bond film. No one but my wife cares whether a little flesh is hanging out here and there. I pull the comforter over my head and drift back to sleep.

> lucky moon –
> even when waning no one
> threatens to replace you

Unsaddled

Breakfast without a newspaper is a horse without a saddle.

~ Edward R. Murrow

I am six months into my experiment of not reading the daily newspaper. So while eating breakfast I read essays, including one by E.B. White who in response to Murrow's metaphor called breakfast, "The hour when we sit munching stale discouragement along with fresh toast."

My days are less angst ridden now, but I sometimes feel I've missed something important - something others know that I don't, but should.

Stretching Murrow's metaphor, it's me that's unsaddled - riderless.

This morning, as I walk the dog on a berm overlooking the freeway, there's the usual tangle of commuters, all hurrying somewhere.

> winter morning -
> the cat mews
> over an empty bowl

Note: Both the Murrow and White quotes are taken from E.B. White, "Newspaper Strike," *The New Yorker*, December 12, 1953.

Muse

In the dimly lit Japanese restaurant. I glance at my watch and grumble to myself: *Must have gotten the time wrong.*

As I gaze absently at the paintings on the walls, the petite almond-eyed waitress approaches, looks at the empty chair:

"Friend come soon?"

"Yes, soon," I reply.

A half-hour later, I catch her eye.

"Not coming. Ohhhh . . . so sorry. Want order?"

Yes, some sort of order has been lost and I want it back. Without the steady rhythm of work, I evidently no longer know which day of the week it is.

A thin volume of poetry open, I stuff down noodles and words, pretend that I'm not one to be pitied, but instead admired for being able to live so rich a solitary life.

> next to the
> flickering candle –
> an origami goat

Note: As it happens, the number of folds made in crafting an origami goat corresponded closely to my age at the time the author had this experience.

What Are You Up To?

The sun's rays filter through a stand of black spruce where 20 horses are hitched. Dave, a lanky outfitter, and I are unpacking them. We chat about the grizzly we spotted earlier in the day and how the horses are holding up.

> men's talk –
> the smell of sweat
> and manure

Dave asks, "Ray, what are you up to these days?"

I'm embarrassed to say that I receive a monthly check without having to work, that I no longer wake up by an alarm clock, that I feel guilty about those who have to rush breakfast and fight traffic, that I view my avocations as luxuries in a world stressed by war and poverty.

Finally I say: "Well, I write a bit and do some photography."

Dave replies, "Oh, do you sell your photographs?"

"Some, but not enough to pay for the camera."

So there it is. I can't simply sit on the back stoop and admire the lawn growing, the shadows lengthening.

"Well," Dave grunts as he hefts a 60-pound load off the horse, "must be nice to have time to pursue your interests."

How many times have I heard that I now have time to be the writer I always wanted to be, to travel as much as I want?

The horses don't like being corralled, and I don't either.

In younger times I was "a jock," "a professional," "a dad," "a leader" and "a teacher." Now I'm "a retiree," "a senior," "grey bearded," all of which carry undertones of "geezer," hints of "useless."

We release the horses and they race out of the corral, roll in the black loam, shake and begin to graze.

I wish this rawness I feel could as easily be shaken off.

>   monkshood bloom –
>   the whine of mosquitoes
>   seems diminished

Stolen Memories

Midnight, the unlit windows of homes, a whisper of wind, the rustle of leaves. In a back alley, I scramble over a wooden fence, intent on stealing apples.

The yard I enter was my first home after graduating from college. My father always had apple trees, so when he visited me, he bought and helped me plant the tree whose bounty I plan to plunder. On our knees, side by side, we tamped earth over the tree's roots.

I pick an apple and take a bite. Its crisp tartness takes me back to the taste of his rust-striped Gravensteins, to the aroma of baked apples and pies.

He died ten years ago. A year later I sold this house. I have a tree in my new backyard, but not the tree that we planted.

> windfall –
> a basket full
> of memories

Storyteller

My eight-year-old tags along behind, making up stories as we wind our way along the trail to Peek-A-Boo Springs. Elldorn, who I gather is an elf, seems to be having trouble with Buckwart.

I drift in and out of her story, from time to time inserting an "uh, huh" while enjoying the sandstone pinnacles, an occasional claret cup cactus in bloom, the trill of a canyon wren.

"So what do you think Elldorn should do, Dad?"

"Um, maybe he should fight him."

"Dad! Elldorn is a girl."

"Well . . . I meant she should fight him. Elf against goblin."

"Dad!! Buckwart is a dwarf. He's her best friend."

"Ah, yeah, um, perhaps they should fight them."

"Dad!!! They're trying to help the feather people find a new home."

emerging
from a patch of sand –
sweet vetch

Dusky Moments

Free of the Canadian winter, I float into the warm, transparent waters of Saint Croix. Yellow-finned Blue Tangs and Black-striped Angelfish flow like butterflies through the reef while feeding on algae. A tiny Dusky Damselfish patrols its private patch and drives off invaders by feigning attacks and nipping them.

Later, while relaxing with a beer at my favorite beachside pub, a mob of brightly garbed tourists flow off their cruise ship to graze the shops and cafés. As my private nook fills with commotion, I fire off a stream of silent invective: "What a Loudmouth," "He looks like a beached white whale," "Where did she get those horrible shorts?"

But that raven-haired woman wearing short shorts and a striped tanktop is allowed to pass without a nip. I consider inviting her for a drink and offering to help her apply more sun lotion.

> scent of patchouli
> on a moonlit beach
> first kiss

Desert Walks

In mountain wilderness, my habit is to walk from sunrise to sunset. Friends suggest that I should pause more and "be in" rather than "move through." But if a meditation serves the spirit, why meddle? Buddhists chant, Dervishes dance, I hike. And a sense of place slips in quietly through body's urban armor.

Noon sun. These desert red rock canyons shimmer with heat waves, trump mind's will to move. Body, wiser than mind, closes down - eyes, nose, ears, skin. And so I travel short distances, stop at pools of water and shade, seek out springs, swim in muddied places shared with tadpoles.

Late afternoon. Sun's glare diminishes, winds whisper and skin opens as to a lover's caress. Frogs sing their lust, bees hum in the fragrant yellow barberry.

And eyes inherited from a people who evolved in the filtered light of forest canopy, once again take in. When only a few hours ago the junipers sagged like dusty tramps, their turquoise berries glow like fireflies and alpenglow lights up sandstone walls.

The desert is dancing in color!

>   land of little water -
>   washed clean
>   by the walking

Pathways

Despite portents of rain, several companions
and I make a slow, step-by-step ascent to
Persimmon Peak. Sunlight bursts now and then
through gray-black cumulus clouds.
In the treeless, alpine region, wildflowers that
have evolved into miniatures to cope with the
strong winds and sparse soils - white bistort,
yellow cinquefoil, purple harebells - radiate
color.

After a rest on top, we descend on a steep scree
slope and make the long walk back to camp. I
limp along behind on a petulant ankle.

*Will I care when I'm no longer able to hike like
this? How much of my imagined self is in the doing
of it? Who would I be without that doing?*

Perhaps answers will come during tonight's
campfire with the sharing of poetry and wine.

> tiny white bistort -
> do you imagine yourself
> a wild rose?

To Be a Man

The blizzard brings a stranger in through the door of our cook tent. He gathers himself in close by the wood stove, drops run off his stained, well-worn Stetson. The red hot stovepipe casts a rose color on a face scarred from a wolf's mauling.

"It's Mike," he says, reaching out a calloused hand for a shake and a swig of the offered bottle of rye. He tells us that he's 78 and used to be a bull rider. "An I jus' had prostit surjry, plumin' weren't wurkin', now it wurks one way but not t'other."

"How is it to be out of the loving business?" someone asks.

"Jus' like steppin' off a buckin' bull, peaceful like an' damn sure glad to still be walkin'."

The next day brings in three more hunters. We hunch in close by the stove, each in turn spewing the bull—a grizzly encounter; a horse stepping off a cliff; an angry moose that thrashed down a tree before it was shot.

I have stories too but don't tell them. What makes for this reluctance, this distance I feel from these men's men? Is it because I'm usually on foot and not riding a horse? That I'm not a hunter? Never rodeoed? Never worked the land with hands and back?

> burn of straight whiskey –
> my only scar
> surgical

A Glimpse of the Moon

Every so often, Brianna and I leave our different cities and journey together on a holiday. We've just arrived at a small inn on the Oregon Coast to enjoy the ocean and spring wildflowers. While she showers, I lay in bed browsing a collection of Yoshitoshi's woodblocks. "A Glimpse of the Moon," shows a man, his face masked by a fan, peeking over a wicker fence at a geisha slipping out of her pink, floral-patterned kimono for an evening bath.

> wild rose –
> a tiny dark spider
> waiting beneath

I peek over the top of my book as Brianna stands by the window brushing her hair. In moonlit silhouette, she turns, slides off her robe, turns and slowly walks the distance that separates us.

In the morning, I show her the woodblock and confess that I enjoyed watching her undress.

In the morning, I show her the woodblock and confess that I enjoyed watching her undress. "And I enjoyed you watching," she says as she pulls off the covers.

> floating
> to the ground –
> wild rose petals

Note: "A Glimpse of the Moon," by the late ukiyo-e master Tsukioka Yoshitoshi (1839 – 1892), is number 37 of his woodblock print series, "One Hundred Aspects of the Moon."

At a Friend's Cottage

A cardinal's song has drawn me out for a walk through stands of maples, hemlocks and birch. In a small clearing I come across a one-room cottage with "Our Home" painted over the entry. Windows broken, door hanging askew on a single hinge, it's now a shelter for mice and squirrels.

The residents were settlers who arrived in the 1890s, cut and milled the trees into lumber, built the cottage, over-farmed the marginal soil, and moved on. A flowering peony just outside the window was likely bought at great expense to remind them of the old country.

The interior room is lit by sun streaming through a crisscross of broken roof beams. Stained walls are decorated with barely legible posters: sheep and mountains in the Scottish Highlands; a farm family riding in a horse drawn wagon on a bright summer day; and a sailing ship, perhaps to take the residents to far away places, or back to their native land.

> day dreams –
> tatters of paper
> hanging from a wall

Red Man Ruin

Birds sing us awake. The sun is painting the canyon walls a soft orange. We spread our map on the camp table, slurp strong tea, munch toast smeared with peanut butter and jam, and head out. Two hours later, we enter the steep sandstone walls of Lost Canyon. And someone calls out, "Look, up there, on the left!"

There's a rectangular shadow indicating the doorway of a structure built by the Anasazi 1000 years ago. Otherwise invisible, it's made with flat stones held together by a cement-like mud that still shows indentations made by their finger tips. Scattered about are pottery shards and small corncobs. Above the ruin is a pictograph of a humanoid figure painted in red.

We climb further up onto the canyon rim where more structures are likely to be hidden. Near the top, someone says: "Look, over there!" We've come across three ruins with firewood laid out as if prepared for tonight's fire, as if we've just returned from the hunt.

Thirsty, coated with dried sweat and dust, we return to camp. Someone says: "Did you hear that Martin has lung cancer?" Martin who hiked with us years ago. I search my memory: Did he smoke? Was there a wife? Children?

As we talk, bits and pieces of the man emerge from shadow - the shards and corncobs of a life.

> campfire talk -
> light flickers among
> the shadows

Possibilities

Springtime in Utah. For several weeks, I woke to the song of a tiny black and white warbler, shared a pancake breakfast with my hiking companions, and considered the possibilities.

From sunup to sunset, we explored a labyrinth of canyons, came across thousand-year-old Anasazi ruins built into sandstone walls, mused about the meaning of their evocative rock art. By firelight, we shared dinner, drank spirits and watched the moon rise above sandstone spires.

Back home in Canada, I wake to the sound of house sparrows chattering in the still leafless apple tree, pour milk over dry cereal and consider the possibilities. Read the newspaper? Go shopping? Clean the garage? Pay the bills? At 1 p.m. I have a dental appointment.

> my bicycle
> resting against the wall –
> both tires flat

The Whole Works

Five p.m. I don my knapsack and head out on the trail.
I meet a backpacker speeding along toward the
trailhead. He's young, has brush cut hair and, the stuff
of envy, a shirtless turtle belly.

He opens with: "Neat place!"

"Yeah, sure is," I reply. "How long have you been out?"

"Three days, long enough to see everything."

"Everything?" The question jumps out of my mouth—as
much a challenge as a surprise.

"Yeah, Lost Canyon, Druid Arch, Chesler Park, the Joint
Trail, rock art, ruins - the whole works."

"Wow, that's quite a hike in only three days," I say. I'm
thinking that in my 25 years of hiking in this labyrinth of
sandstone canyons I haven't yet seen 'the whole works.'

As in a mirror, I see myself in him - a young man full
of enthusiasm to hike all the trails, see all the places.
"So, where are you headed?" he asks.

"I'm going into that small wash," I say, gesturing towards
a non-descript branch of the main canyon.

"Oh, What's in there?"

Maybe he's hoping that I'll say that the wash contains an Anasazi ruin or an arch. Anything will do, so long as it has a name to designate its collectability. How to tell him?

There's no great feature in the place I've selected for this evening's walk. It's one of many small places where an occasional rush of water shapes sandstone walls into delicate curves, where desert plants offer unexpected splashes of color, where the only water in small pot holes contain brine shrimp and tadpoles, where stunted junipers twist and twirl in the dance of life and where there will likely be no footprints besides my own.

"Nothing much, I'm just wandering around."

"Oh," he says. "Well, have a good one!"

I've stepped to the other side of the mirror, seeing myself through his eyes—sparse hair, graying beard, weathered shirt, scuffed boots, waistline bulge - the whole works.

"You too," I reply, and might have added, *You have a good, full life. There's plenty of time for you to learn to walk in the beauty of small places.*

> alpenglow -
> the long shadow cast
> by a pebble

Lucky Day

Morning started with a rainstorm, but now the sun streams through my office window. Along with the sun, I'm blessed with two emails. Mr. Tony Emumelu of the Zenith Bank of Nigeria informs me that I've inherited $14.6 million from someone who isn't even a relative. And 23-year-old Betsy Johnson has asked me to become her pal on Romance.com. Of our planet's 6.6 billion candidates, both chose me!

After a brief struggle between greed and romance, I renounce the prospect of becoming one of the world's richest men and choose a relationship with Betsy.

Why not take both? Because I wouldn't know whether Betsy only wants me for my money.

On Betsy's pal site, I learn that in order to consummate our relationship, it will cost $5/month for a premium membership. So I ask Mr. Emumelu whether he will spot me the fee if I sign the remainder of the $14.6 million over to him.

> monthly bills –
> a cuckoo's egg
> in the warbler's nest

Winter Retreat

The cabin rental is a gift from a friend, a place to mull over retirement. Tucked away in a spruce forest, I reach it after travelling hours on a dirt and gravel road.

As I put groceries in the fridge, I spot a note posted near the coffee maker: "Join the family. Add your mug."

The mugs are ceramic and glass, patterned and plain, large and small. I'm tempted to borrow one showing a clock with no hands and "Who cares, I'm retired" printed on it, but instead use the plastic cup I picked up at Tim Horton's.

On my afternoon walk along an ice-crusted creek, I happen on another mug collection hanging like ornaments in the branches of a birch tree. A cracked teapot rests nearby on a stone.

Warming myself later by the stone fireplace, the guestbook informs me that the mugs are retired, belonging to guests who have not returned.

I drift off thinking of the teapot, sitting alone, as if waiting to be used.

> new year's eve –
> candlelight flickers
> on knotty pine

A Long Walk

Nine p.m., my three-hour class is finished. On the way to my car, I pass along a near-deserted block of food venues and shops.

Coffee? . . . too late.

Cookies? . . . too many calories.

Newspaper? . . . too depressing.

The Atlantic Magazine? . . . too tired to read it.

Artwork? . . . the swirl of color in "The Kiss" isn't for my wall.

Valentine display? . . . none for the old man in the reflection.

Book? . . . I pass on *Playmates of 1965*. Let young men worship paper women.

On impulse, I buy Graham Greene's *A Life in Letters* and head home.

> rust spots –
> the starter motor's
> grinding noise

Late into the night, Greene reveals his loves, betrayals and struggles with depression. And then I find: "Cure the disease and I doubt whether a writer would remain."

What's in a Name?

I'm one of 16 recipients of an e-mail from the woman with whom I had broken up several months earlier. I wonder about the others whose e-mail addresses include:

Twitterful@. . . I think of him as a 'twit.'

CuzIsezso@. . . Typical guy. Where does she find them?

Armyguy@. . . Does he do pushups while making love?

TopDog@. . . How will this work? It was her that liked being on top.

Perhaps I'll change my email address to Trashed@. . .

     fall drizzle . . .
     my finger poised
     above the delete key

Falling

Midnight. I wake up in her candle-lit bedroom, our bodies cupped, my hand resting on her breast. She snuggles closer, says, "Again?" And after, "Stay tonight."

In the dream, small black dogs turn somersaults and jump through fiery hoops. The spotlit high-wire artist with a red-sequined woman balanced on his shoulders takes a tentative step. Below, a clown cavorts with a butterfly net to catch them when they fall.

> 3 a.m. –
> kicking loose
> the too-tight blankets

Catching Up

On my bike, I approach the steep hill I've learned to hate. And an image of a gray-bearded man comes to mind. We met 30 years ago at the trailhead for the climb to the 14,000-foot summit of Mt. Whitney.

"Going up?" I had asked him.

"Not for me anymore," he replied.

As I grudgingly peddle up at a slow pace, I remember thinking that that one day I'd be him. But not today!

Half-way up, I shoulder check and see a gold and red spandex kid bulleting up behind me. Determined not to let him pass, I turn on as much speed as I can muster. At the top, he gives me a thumbs up, satisfying, not because he acknowledged my victory, but because he was also breathing hard.

> sunny morning –
> beardless
> after a close shave

Chest Pains!

A voice in my mind says, "Get it checked," but the one that likes the lawn to get quite long before mowing it, says: "Just a muscle spasm, don't worry about it."

One day passes, two, three . . . seven now. The pain has ebbed and flowed, but not gone away. The possibilities dance through my mind: heart attack, cancer, ulcer, kidney stone, gall bladder - the list goes on and on. And I drive to EMERGENCY.

The triage nurse asks how long I've had the pains. I only confess to two days. She pats my hand: "You mustn't wait when you have chest pains. We'll take you next."

"NEXT!" Who gets immediate attention in an emergency ward? I imagine metal tongs prying my chest open, a quadruple by-pass (whatever that is), a dead person's heart jammed into my chest cavity.

Soon, I'm fitted into one of those tiny hospital gowns with too many personal parts showing. The medical workers draw blood, read blood pressure, administer an ECG.

WAITING. Minutes seem like hours. White coats pass by, but none stop. Have they forgotten me? Or, better, perhaps they've decided to ignore me because there's no immediate problem. My imagination's evil doctor, the one with the pencil line moustache and snide smile, whispers to the charge nurse: *As punishment for waiting seven days, let him sit for a few more hours.*

And the "Is it too late" thoughts stream in: *I should have done my will, pre-paid the funeral home, hugged my kids more, told someone I was coming in, eaten a last meal.*

I'm startled by the sound of a monitor flatlining, consider getting dressed and bolting out the door. I imagine orderlies dragging me back, the triage nurse's 'tut-tut' as they lash me to a stretcher.

And then, the REAL DOCTOR arrives, scans the paperwork, says: "All clear. Guess you had a bit of a scare, eh? Next time come in right away."

> Viagra TV Ad –
> twenty elderly men dance
> in the street

Church Going

On occasion, I enter a church to escape the everyday world. The denomination doesn't matter – just that there's no service and that the door is unlocked.

The thin light passing through stained glass windows and musty smells bring to mind Saint Barnabas Grammar School where we started each morning with the Mass.

I remember the dour countenance of Sister Angelica during catechism class: "Raymond, what is the purpose of the life of man?" If I failed to answer correctly that, "The purpose of the life of man is to know and love God," I'd have to hold out my palms for slaps from her ruler.

The boy's purpose: *to avoid getting his hands slapped.*

The statue of Mary with open arms reminds me of Sister Theresa who gave a lonely boy empty pill bottles for his insect collection.

Her purpose: *to do a bit of good where one is able.*

Recently I learned of her death. Long ago, I should have sent a thank you note.

A man's purpose: *to shoulder the regrets.*

> coins clatter
> into the collection box –
> waxing moon

Notes: The title is taken from Philip Larkin's poem "Church Going." A reminder that I once visited churches late at night came from Lawrence Block's character, Matthew Scudder.

Continental Divide

Wendy, freckle-faced, hair in pigtails and intense blue eyes, says: "I'd like to hike with you today."

We follow Persimmon Creek, pass waterfalls and alble through fields of alpine buttercups as we make our way to the top of the Continental Divide where mountain peaks jut up on all sides .

On our return, we race down a steep scree slope in long jumps. We come to a small waterfall with a pool deep enough for a swim—a spot I've had in mind all day. I gesture toward the pool and Wendy takes the hint and undresses. As she enters, she looks back over her shoulder with a Mona Lisa smile: "You can look, but don't touch."

Stripping off the clothing that covers this old man's body, I follow her into the pool: "And, you can touch, but don't look."

> handful
> of cool water -
> one thirst quenched

Cybercafe

It's been four weeks since I struck out for the wilderness of Southern Utah. Each day, I've loaded my pack with food, water and camera and headed off to photograph sandstone canyon landscapes.

Today I need supplies, drive to a small town and enter a small cafe. It's a kaleidoscope of the senses: new age music, smells of coffee and home-baked goods, visions of down-to-earth 70s garb. Crafts and artwork decorate walls and cabinets. A bulletin board offers massage, acupuncture, palm readings and tai chi.

A number of us ply computers. I don't speak except to order coffee and food, yet I feel connected, as if we solo travelers have each used a different path to find our way to this shared oasis.

Email floods in—messages from friends and a wave of spam offering sexual aids and the companionship of wanton females. It feels like I'm a 19th century sailor arriving at an island port, receiving mail from home and anticipating the favours of exotic women.

The messages rest in my mind like the flotsam and jetsam found on a beach—glad tidings and troubling news. I am torn by the urge to rush home to the complexities of everyday life and the desire to return to the simple elegance of the canyons.

> desert streambed –
> a scatter of debris from
> the last flash flood

Dear Birdwatcher

I found your name listed as the local president of the Edmonton Bird Society. I know the robin is one of the most melodic of the thrush family and that I should be overwhelmed with pleasure by its morning ode to joy. But why, I wonder, can't the bird sing at a more decent hour when people are already up and about? And why can't I have a hermit thrush instead? From its name, I assume that it's solitary and less likely to trumpet its songs at 4:30 a.m.

This morning I've been pondering solutions. What about a trail of breadcrumbs from my back yard to the neighbor's - the woman who releases her yappy, rodent-sized dogs at precisely 6:30 a.m. Why not let my robin bugle her awake?

And what, you might be wondering, do you have to do with this? A bit of advice, please. What type of breadcrumbs should I use: plain, garlic or arsenic-laced?

> dark clouds -
> the robin gulps down
> my raspberries

Descending

"A man descending is propelled by inertia; the only initiative left him is whether or not he decides to enjoy the passing scene."

~ Guy Vanderhaeghe

Outside, snowflakes swirl and drift, while inside the fire sizzles. Eliza Gilkyson's "The Party's Over" is playing in the background. My friend is reading a novel she "can't put down."

I say, "Eliza's right. The party is over. I'm just taking up space."

"What!" She protests: "You're speaking of yourself as if you're a parasite, but I see you as a man of passion with many interests."

"Don't most people my age think that their life lacks meaning?" I reply. "I watch too much bland TV, read too much pulp fiction."

"But you do photography, write stories, make deep trips into wilderness, bring others along, teach people to write," she insists.

"I'm a dabbler," I say. "Dabbler ducks don't dive deep; they simply tip their tails up and feed in the shallows."

"Why isn't it enough to just be?" she wants to know. "Why not savor our frittata and wine, the warmth of the fire, our companionship?"

"I do feel blessed that a talented woman like you is willing to share so many things with me in the fall of my life," I reply.

"I guess anyone like me would do then . . . you're just dabbling with me."

"How did we get to you and me?" I ask.

> snow flurries –
> windows
> coated with ice

Cinnamon Bark

"... the trinket aunts always had a little something in their pocketbooks, cinnamon bark or a penny or nickel ..."
~ A.R. Ammons, Excerpt from "Easter Morning"

When my mother's immigrant parents and siblings died of the Spanish flu, her uncles and aunts didn't take her in. She became an orphanage girl who scrambled with the other children for the pennies and nickels thrown on the ground by well-meaning visitors on holidays.

When I was a child, she sang and made us treats. "You look hungry," she'd say at dinnertime while heaping more pasta on my plate. "Mangia! Mangia!" Cinnamon bark pasta, I'd call it now.

We visit mom for Easter dinner in her resident home. "Mom," my sister says, "look how they've done your hair. It's so beautiful." It doesn't look any different to me than that of the many other gray-haired residents.

Mom is trying to shuffle something off her plate and looking toward me. I can sense her wanting to pass something to me, some bits of cinnamon bark.

> her hair
> a gray halo -
> lullaby memories

Dover Beach & My Backyard

My daughter is just finishing the spring yard work. The raked lawn already shows hints of green and her black-and-white cat is sunning. A flutter of wings lets me know that the red-breasted nuthatches have once again returned to the birdhouse.

A book open to Matthew Arnold's poem "Dover Beach" rests on my chest as I sway back and forth in the hammock. The newspaper with headlines about the Middle East is cast aside.

Arnold portrays the world as "a darkling plain" where "ignorant armies clash by night." He likens the loss of faith in his era to the "withdrawing roar of a retreating sea."

Is my faith lost? No. I believe that mosquitoes will hatch all too soon, that at any moment, the cat will make a try on the nuthatches and the dog will arrive to nag me to toss the ball. And I'm certain that an army of dandelions will soon march across the lawn.

> storm clouds gathering –
> a robin's
> evening song

Endings

On our morning walk, we're rewarded with an emerald pond fringed with cattails. There's a bench on a small rise from which to view the ducks, loons and grebes. A brass plaque attached to the bench reads:

Soggy Dog Lake
named by Betty Martin who liked this place.

I imagine a curly-haired dog prancing out of the lake, then shaking and showering Betty and her initial dismay followed by laughter.

Before leaving, we lay a wildflower on her bench.

The trail back curves gently through stands of pine and poplar. My companion, walking just ahead, favors a chronically sore hip. "I may not be able to do this much longer," she says.

> through a
> dark bus window –
> a wave goodbye

Day's End

Oceans once filled this arid land and then receded, leaving deposits of salt and layers of hardened sand. Rivers next carved deep canyons and rich bottom soils in which humans built shelters, hunted and grew crops. And then came a 100-year drought.

Tonight a waning moon rises left of Orion. My tent sits where the Anasazi grew corn, squash and beans. Their stone shelters look as if they were built yesterday. Now empty but for the occasional pack rat or black widow, painted handprints float like ghosts above entryways. Pottery shards and corn cobs are scattered about.

Here and there, in these meandering canyons, I find springs too small to have nourished the Old Ones. I've brought food, water and shelter with me. All this sufficient to sustain one man.

> winter wind
> in my silvered hair –
> good fortune, and for what?

Note: The title and phrase "good fortune, and for what" and the idea for this haibun are taken from a translation of a poem by Tu Fu (712-770) a prominent Chinese poet of the Tang Dynasty.

Family Tree

My chain saw has reduced the once graceful birch to a scatter of rounds. I gather barrow after barrow, set them on the chopping block and ply my axe.

On the largest round, I trace the rings back to the year we moved in, the year each daughter left, and the year of the divorce. The ring at the edge marks my mother's death.

family gathering –
the incinerator door
clanks shut

This winter friends will join me for wine and poetry by a warming fire. I'll feed the white-bark wood, piece-by-piece, into the fireplace. But tonight, it's just me.

embers and ash –
the slow burn of
aged whiskey

More or Less

More than once, she said that she wanted more. I wasn't sure what she meant, and didn't ask. I hadn't told her that, if anything, I wanted less.

Four months ago she said, "I'm ending it. I hope that in the future we can still be friends."

It's been a long winter without the companionship and sensual pleasures we shared. Then yesterday, she wrote that she wants to get together for dinner at "our" restaurant and afterwards at her place for dessert.

I wonder, does she want to try again and is willing to settle for what we had?

And what do I want?

> ripples on the lake –
> the dog fetches
> another stick

Last Class

As if washed in by a wave, a surge of students enters and the room fills with sound. I introduce a case study and am delighted by their intelligence as we discuss it. But I'm also disappointed as I perceive that they clearly haven't prepared, are already finished with this term's work.

Near the end of the three hours, the pace slackens and there's a lull like the one when the tide stops running in and begins to run out. I see fatigue in their faces, understand their need to exit these stiff-backed plastic seats, this stuffy room, and get on with what's next in their lives.

I congratulate them on completing the course and ask those who are graduating to stand. "You've worked hard for this," I say, "You shouldn't just leave as if nothing significant has happened." And we applaud them.

They stand, gather books and hurry from the room. A few stop to thank me for the course.

I shut down the projector, shovel papers into my briefcase, hear myself mumbling that I'm graduating too, that this is the last class I will teach. I am unable to blink away the tears.

> silence -
> chairs occupied
> by a thousand ghosts

Life after Floss

After lunch I wander into the bathroom and, blast it, I can't remember whether I'd flossed this morning. And I worry that other things are slipping away.

Just last week while picking away at the plaque, my dental hygienist led off with, "Do you floss every morning and evening?"

Why ask? She already knows the answer. I suspect she's deliberately careless with the pick because I'd scheduled my yearly visit a bit late . . . *okay 18 months late*. I dare not deflect with "I donno, I forget" because Ms. Dominatrix's pick is poised for further punishment.

Just as past generations of parents tried to encourage good behavior by warning their children of the boogeyman, she too predicts gloom and doom. Were she more adept at cautionary tales, she might model the practices of the clergy who scared boys with the threat that masturbation leads to blindness, or worse, causes hair to grow on the palms of the sinner's hands. I remember keeping my hands in my pockets for an entire week for fear that their meanderings in the shower would reveal what I'd been up to.

So should I floss now when I may already have? Were I to lose a tooth before something else goes, would it be so bad? If that's all I lose in the next few years, I'll feel blessed.

> a steady drizzle
> from morning to night -
> mispeled words

Birds of a Flock

I zoom my lens on two teens sitting hunched against a peeling stucco wall. Costumed in frayed jeans, dirty T-shirts and unlaced sneakers, they're watching the milling crowd of revelers at the festival I've come to photograph. Both have tattoos and burn marks on their arms. Their faces are masked with a studied blankness.

Like a flock of birds moving in unison, the crowd veers around them.

The one with the word "Mystery" written on his black T-shirt catches me snapping his picture and gives me "the look." It's a look I'd learned to quickly retreat from in the voilence-prone schools I attened.

I turn and scurry away while wondering whether his gaze might be curiosity rather than the malevolence I'd imagined.

I consider approaching him and saying, *Nice T-shirt, what's the mystery?* Anything to engage him in conversation, to move beyond the stereotype. Instead I do my best to become one of the flock.

> dark alley –
> a black cat
> stalking sparrows

In the Mood

Midday at riverside. Filtered light floats to the forest floor. Poplar leaves hang limp in the heat. Two mallards float along with the languid current.

The mottled female pokes about, dabbles for her dinner, ignores the drake's soft, persistent rasps.

Evening, a candlelit restaurant. Above the hum of voices, Louis Armstrong croons, "I'm in the mood for love."

        wine glasses touch –
        the top button of her blouse
        not undone

Last Walk

I look up, see my daughter's teary eyes. "What's wrong?"

"I think it's time to take Gypsy in," she says.

Our black and white border collie has been with us for 16 years, but she's gone deaf and partly blind. Yesterday, I watched as she hobbled towards her food bowl, her back legs going out from under her. She was stuck half sitting, staring blankly.

Was it only yesterday that she played soccer with the girls in the back yard? She was so fast, it was impossible to kick the ball past her. I let her out now, kick the ball slowly, but she doesn't see it, doesn't move. The red squirrel with which she'd so often enjoyed endless barking wars doesn't bother visiting today.

They go out the door, daughter with dog following along.

Many times leaving for work, I'd look back and see her nose pressed to the window. This time, it's my nose.

> mail delivery –
> the sound of a dog
> not barking

> sunset –
> our cat curled up
> in the dog's bed

Journey to the Far North

The river ice cracks and buckles, ice blocks grind into the bank, twist upward, gouge out black earth, fall back into the torrent.

Mid-river, a female mallard preens on an ice floe. She's a tiny spot of brown, mottled like the dry sedge grasses that will provide cover for her brood under the spring sun.

"Do something, Lady Duck," I yell. "If you just sit there, you'll end up in the Arctic Ocean. Go find your drake."

Back home, my wife says, "Maybe she's the new, emancipated lady duck who's had a glimpse of the trials of raising ducklings in a world of coyotes and hawks."

On the mantle, a photo of our two daughters both drifting toward a world of teen drugs and sex. I want to go back and yell: "Float on, Lady Duck. A solo jaunt to the far north might be just the thing."

> street teen –
> no smile as she calls out
> spare change

Deliverance

Humor—true liberty!—it is you who deliver me from ambition for power, from servitude to party, from respect for routine, from the pedantry of science, from admiration for celebrities, from the mystifications of politics, from the fanaticism of the reformers, from fear of this great universe, and from self-admiration.

~ Proudhon

True liberty, do I have it? As for deliverance from the mystifications of politics, the Conservatives have been in power for 36 years and I badly want to see them defeated. This morning, I count four red and seventeen blue signs on lawns. I release the leashes so that the dogs can visit the blue-signed yards. I tell myself that democracy itself is at stake.

Respect for routine? It's true that I feed the dogs precisely at 7 a.m.; fix breakfast at 7:30; check my email at 8:00, write from 8:00 to noon. But the rest of today is mine, even if it bears a close resemblance to yesterday.

I avoid *People Magazine* while in the dentist's waiting room, so doesn't that stand me well in terms of avoiding admiration for celebrities? On the other hand, I admit to a bit of a fixation on actress Cate Blanchett. Did you see her as the freedom-seeking housewife in *Bandits*, her ethereal grace as Galadriel in *Lord of the Rings*? To my credit, I've not yet sent an offer of marriage.

As for the fanaticism of the reformers, yes, I vote Green. But does that make me a fanatic?

Come humor, deliver me, right this minute, from this fearsome bout of self-admiration. If you fail, I'll have to try meditation.

> first class –
> I begin by examining
> the blonde's navel

Note: The idea and some phrases were borrowed from E.B. White, *Writings from the New Yorker*, 1927-76.

Moonlit Trail

Dusk. The trail curves through a strand of scrub oak. A wicker creel slaps at my side and dried leaves crunch underfoot as I follow along behind my father. I'm proudly carrying my first fishing pole.

At the lakeside, I catch minnows while he baits our hooks and casts far out into the blue-black stillness. We don't talk and I settle into the silence of the night, watch the tip of my pole, await a strike.

As the years pass that silence grows into a great wall between us. Recently, I heard myself saying to a friend, "Not more than twenty words ever passed between my father and me."

Tonight, as I stand beside him, he's strapped into a hospital bed, consumed by dementia. He ruptures the silence with a rant against the doctors and nurses, against the God that's done this to him, and against his family for putting him here.

I think of that long ago lakeside night, of the quiet outdoors man who loved fishing. I want to go back, gently shake him and say, "Speak to your son, speak to him before it is too late."

> the sound of a splash –
> ripples shatter
> the moon's reflection

Note: The idea for this haibun came from William Stafford's poem, "A Certain Bend."

Space Junk

The news under the headline, "Space Junk Keeps Fallin' on My Head," warns that, "If you knew what was going on in the sky, you probably wouldn't sleep at night."

I'm already having sleeping problems. There's the neighbor's barking dog, the cat jumping on the bed at odd hours, nightmares from those dismal news reports I shouldn't read, the resident spider that spirals down from the ceiling just as I'm about to drift into sleep and rehearsing what I might have replied in that last argument with my wife who got in the last word.

Evidently "A whopping 1,217,000 objects, including whole spacecrafts" are ready to plunge to the earth (*and possibly into my home*). Even "a small grain of space dust will be moving so fast" that it can punch through the ceiling and whatever else it hits (*including me*).

So I call NASA to ask whether they can direct one of the objects at the spider who hides every time I reach for the broom. They tell me that the objects fall at random and abruptly hang up.

>   don't worry little spider,
>   NASA has poor
>   customer relations

Note: The haiku is modeled on Issa's "don't worry spider / I keep house / casually."

Moving Day

Reluctantly, I walk through the tiny yard and knock on the door. Joseph opens it and says, "Thanks for coming."

After a somewhat stormy love affair, he and Carmen had decided to "give it a try." She moved in last July. I'm here now to help him move her belongings out. When we finish, he'll change the locks on the doors and she'll receive a letter at work from his lawyer instructing her to not return to the house, to refrain from all future contact, and that her belongings will be found in storage.

Her presence is everywhere, a blouse and scarf hanging on a doorknob, cosmetics in the bathroom, women's magazines on the coffee table. My first task is the bedroom. In the closet, I find her red dancing slippers. "She's an incredible dancer, like a feather in my arms" Joseph once told me.

I try to be respectful by carefully folding her clothing, but know my care won't affect her regard for me when she learns that I've helped. I feel like a silent assassin.

Joseph rails as he works. "She gutted me financially and emotionally. Did you see all those clothes? She was a shopping freak. Bought everything she saw. I'm broke. I have to sell the house."

I try to couple this with his early stories. "Sometimes we were so blessedly hot, we couldn't even make it to the bedroom," he had said.

He fears that she will ignore the lawyer's letter. "Last time we fought, she kicked the door in, then attacked me." He's at the edge of an anxiety attack. "We have to hurry," he says, "she might be here any minute." For a moment, I'm a boy again in the apple orchard, listening for the farmer's footsteps.

As we carry out the final load, I notice a small calendar hanging near the fridge. Thanksgiving day, tomorrow, has been circled in.

Joseph picks up two bricks by the door and locks them in the garage. I raise my eyebrows in a 'What for?' expression.

"The last time we fought, she threw a rock through the window."

> thanksgiving eve –
> the last leaves soon to fall
> from the apple tree

Catalog

Hammacher Schlemmer, self-billed as "America's longest running catalog," arrived in my mailbox today. It claims to offer "the best, the only and the unexpected".

The Automatic Return Putting Cup at $39.95 makes the sound of polite applause when the ball enters the cup. To get my money's worth, I'd prefer one that plays Christina Aguilera's "I am beautiful, no matter what they say," as the ball zips past the cup.

As a boy, I wanted to become a spy, so I seriously consider The G-Man's Convertible Travel Jacket at $69.95 featuring 40 hidden pockets. There are a number of interesting possibilities including a pocket for a pen-weapon. My pen will be filled with poison ink. (Beware, editor, if you turn down this submission!)

I settle on the $49.95 Rotating Globe Running Wheel, which they claim works equally well for hamsters, gerbils and white rats. At the next cocktail party I'm forced to attend, I'll warm up the conversations by relating that my daughter's hamster has circled the globe more than once.

> family day –
> my kids glued
> to computer games

Birch Lake

When I was last here, the lakefront was crowded with families sharing picnic blankets and congregations of teens on beach towels.

I spent most of my time pretending to read while sneaking glances at a particular bikinied girl. I lay on my stomach to hide my lust.

This evening, the grasses are worn from a summer's use and a windfall is spread beneath the apple tree. A bullfrog's "wronk, wronk, wronk" breaks my reverie.

I walk to the nearby lodge and sit alone in the dining room. Several couples dine in silence, staring past one another.

Looking out the window, I see her again, taste that first kiss.

What was her name . . . ?

> mountain sunset –
> painted turtles slumber
> on a weathered log

A Word of Advice

"I have the solution," I say. "And just in time for the visit to your daughter.

"What's that?" she says cautiously.

"You're afraid that you'll ruin things because you can't resist giving her advice. So when you feel the urge, phone me and give me advice instead."

"But I don't have any advice for you."

"Give it a try! What do you have to lose?"

An hour later, she phones back:

"Cut back the peonies and they'll do better next spring."

"Your daughter has peonies?"

"No, but she has house plants."

> wilting
> on my window sill
> African Violets

Another hour passes and there's another call.

"I'm treating you to a new sweater for Christmas."

"You don't like her clothing?"

"She's a ragbag—shops at Goodwill for bargains."

I don't shop at Goodwill and I like my sweater, I'm about
to say, but she's hung up.

>   dangling
>   in the mirror
>   threads from my shirt

Several hours later, another call. I consider not picking up,
but do.

"Your glasses are old-fashioned; they make you look
dated."

"She's twenty-one and wears old-fashioned glasses?"

"No, yours are. And isn't it time for a hearing aid?"

>   falling
>   in the yard
>   the heads of peonies

Moving On

My last day at work. Files dumped into recycle bins; books sent to the library; the computer erased, all ready for the next occupant.

The plants have not fared well. Into the wastebasket go the remains of the Crown of Thorns, a friend's gift when I took over as Department Chair. It likely died during one of those interminable meetings where egos reign and little is accomplished.

Mementos cover one wall including a number of teaching awards. On occasion I run into a middle-aged stranger who holds out a hand and says, "You probably don't remember me, but I had you for a class when I was at university. It was one of the few I enjoyed." I'm touched by these unexpected meetings and manage to say, "Thanks. I hope the class was of use."

In a photo, my wife and two young daughters smile with arms entwined. The teen years wreaked considerable havoc. Perhaps there's still time for reconciliation.

I look out the window, the sun bright on spring's greenery, the jingle of RV keys in my pocket, the camping gear packed.

> a long winter –
> how quickly
> the snow melts

An Empty Place

The woods here seem empty despite the tracks of coyotes, moose, deer and too-many-to-count small critters. Minutes ago I filled the bird feeder and the sky quickly filled with feathered life.

The red-capped woodpecker dominates, next in line, a pair of white-breasted nuthatches, their rapier-like beaks perhaps a threat to the chickadees waiting their turn. The chickadees are fluttering about like leaves in the wind, choosing their moment to feed, but red-cap returns and drives them off (god, how I hate bullies!).

I've lived much of my life like these feathered butterflies, avoiding the bullies, hiding out, picking my moments, wishing I had punched red-headed Jack Renner when he was torturing one of the smaller kids.

> scatter of sunflower
> shells - empty
> feeder

I'm feeling empty too, but I'll sail this paper airplane out into the poetryland, where so many others are fluttering about.

Weighing In

"You tend to notice the strawberry tart in Kronville's Café a lot more when your diet forbids you to have any."
~ Philip Kerr, *The Pale Criminal*

At our last men's meeting, we agreed to weigh in. To our surprise, two of us were in the obese range and two were somewhere between overweight and obese.

Tonight, the guys are back over for steak and beer. Alex says he's cutting back to one beer and going on a diet. Bob says he's been dieting for a month, and he's lost three pounds since our last meeting. Michael, who isn't dieting, has brought one of his homemade apple pies and my eyes are locked on the four quarters he's just carved out. I'm on a low carb diet, and having lost four pounds, I've inched a bit closer to 'normal' than 'obese.' When I announce that I'm no longer a member of the almost obese club, they closely eye what I'm eating, and so I'm having to avoid the tomato-cheese casserole and the garlic French bread.

Bob says, "I read that people are living longer lives if they control their weight."
I reply, "But what kind of living?"
He says, "My uncle is doing quite well at 84."
I ask, "How well does he get around?"
Bob admits that his uncle, "shuffles, but he's happy."
"Happy doing what?"
"Well, he doesn't do much, but he reads and his mind is active."

"I'm not dieting to live longer," I say. "I don't want to be 84."

Bob says, "You could be doing quite well at 84, look how healthy you are, how much hiking you do and bicycling around the city."

While he's stretching my truth, I'm thinking that maybe I'll strip off my shirt and show them my unturtle-like belly and love handles.

"How much extra do you get to eat if you walk for an hour?" Alex asks, while sipping his third beer and taking a second quarter of the pie, the piece that might have been mine.

"About 250 calories if you walk fast," Bob says.

"Is that equal to a slice of pie?" Alex asks.

Bob gets out his calorie counter, holds his thumb and forefinger close together and says, maybe a sliver this big.

> far horizon –
> a sliver
> of moon

Mullings

Revenge is a dish best served cold.

I sit in darkness but for the glow of smouldering fireplace embers. Sipping from an almost empty bottle of cheap red wine first opened a week ago, I read an article that suggests we derive feelings of well being from how closely our friendship abilities match those of our friends. So I send Bob an email:

> Dear Bob, Had I rated myself as a "1" on the friendship ability scale, you would rate as a suitable friend. But I rated myself at "9" (modesty prevented me from using a "10") and you at "1", so we're not a good match. You're likely thinking that this has to do with Linda dumping me, but let me assure you that it doesn't. She too rates a "1", roughly the equivalent to that of a Slime Mold. This explains why you two are doing so well.

The next day, I receive a complaint from the Slime Scientist Society. Their woolly-headed biologist claims that I've unfairly stereotyped Slime Molds, and were I to open my mind, I'd find they play an important ecological role in the decomposition of organic material. I reply that I am well aware of their value since I had only to open my fridge after Linda left to see them playing their vital role. I wonder whether Bob put them onto me.

winter storm –
the acrid taste
of stale wine

Recovery

How strange for tears to well up while pushing a cart through the linoleum aisles of a grocery store. Is this because I'm once again on my feet after three bedridden weeks with this season's influenza? Or is it more related to the fear I felt that I might not make it?

The rattle of shopping cart wheels brings me back to the task at hand: soup for the return of appetite. While sick, I often thought of the thin broth that my mother brought to my bedside when I was sick.

But feeling much better, I discover an array of mouth-watering offerings: butternut squash, ginger carrot, sweet potato, mulligatawny, creamy potato leek.

> sweet melon soup –
> the anticipation
> of my lover's kiss

Monk's Journey

Outside, apple blossoms glow in the dusk. She lies on her side, head propped up on a pillow, her eyes telling me that something important is about to be said, my eyes taking in the candlelight on her breasts.

> courtesan and monk,
> we sleep under one roof together,
> moon in a field of clover

"I need to know more about you," she says.

"Do you mean about being a monk?"

"Yes, because right now you don't seem very much like a monk." She glances at my hand wandering along the curve of her hip.

"You're thinking about Christian monks, the ones who lived in dank cells, ate lentils and hard bread; the ones who whipped themselves. Think instead of Basho, the Japanese monk who traveled extensively, shared his poetry with peasants and samurai nobles, loved flowers, enjoyed the company of women. Think more of a European troubadour with haiku as his song."

> I'm a wanderer
> so let that be my name,
> the first winter rain

"Does this mean that I'm just someone who happens to sleep with you?"

"No, but I've been a partner all of my life, and for now I need not to be."

"So what am I, then?" she asks. "I don't know how to tell my friends whatever it is we're doing. It feels like more than dating or having sex and it's not friendship because I don't sleep with my friends."

> how reluctantly
> the bee emerges from deep
> within the peony

"Can't we simply enjoy what we have," I reply.

"I'm reluctant to give up the feel of your skin against mine, but I'll have to think about this." She pecks a kiss, dresses and leaves.

A week later her note arrives: "I have such good memories of our moments together. It's a gift to desire and be desired, but we need such different things."

> winter seclusion –
> sitting propped against
> the same worn post

Note: All haiku are by Basho whose translators include R.H. Blyth, W.J. Higginson, J. Reichhold and Sam Hamill.

Age of Enlightenment

The Greek astronomer Eratosthenes determined that the earth is a sphere and calculated its rough circumference in the third century BC. By the 15th century, most educated people in Europe had abandoned the notion of a flat Earth.

Enlightenment on the matter only came to me this week when I purchased a 15-speed silver bicycle with narrow tires that had the look of being very fast. But as it turns out, little in my prairie city is flat. Even small inclines constrain my speed to just above a slow walk.

I can't be blamed for not knowing. Mostly I've viewed the city through the windows of cars and there's no ocean nearby. The ancients who were in the know so long before me lived near the sea where they could see the tall ships approaching, their sails appearing first on the horizon.

On today's ride, two kids zip past on an uphill yelling "Almost there, Geezer!"

> hitchhiking mosquitos –
> today it's a transfusion I need,
> not a withdrawal

Trying It On

"I feel so comfortable with you," she says, her hand lightly brushing my chest.

Comfortable! I try wearing the word. It's like my bathrobe that long ago should have been rag-bagged, soft and warm, yet full of holes. Or like the overstuffed chair that Dad fell asleep in while watching golf on TV.

"Comfortable!" I protest. "How about instead, 'When I'm with you I feel like a bird about to spiral up into the sky?' Or maybe, 'With you, I feel like a matador dancing with a flame-snorting bull?' Or better yet, 'I love the tension I feel when you take off your biker boots and I see that cobra etched on your big toe nail?'"

"But you don't have a motorcycle," she replies. "And let me have a look at that toenail."

She's smiling as she caresses that place just below my beltline, the uncomfortable zone where my stomach bulges more than I want it to, where her dinner rests so comfortably.

midnight –
passing the tattoo parlor
three times

fall drizzle –
a motorcycle catalogue
arrives in the mail

Caught Out

"Too much sanity may be madness. And maddest of all, to see life as it is and not as it should be."
~ Cervantes, Don Quixote

Reader. You've caught me here, cowering in a tiny spot of shade at the bottom of a 1200-foot-deep canyon, in the only shade I've been able to find while hiking back to my truck at the top.

The temperature is 105 degrees. Well, I admit that a thermometer would say that it's a mere 80 degrees. But thermometers have no feelings and I do, so I added 25 degrees to represent the fact that I feel as if the sun is carroming off the canyon walls like a fiery cannonball.

You, reader, are likely thinking that something is wrong here, that were I a John Muir, Henry Thoreau or Edward Abbey, I'd be likening this place to the eating of a succulent peach. And yes, when I squint through the undulating heat waves, I can see that twisting cottonwood, its yellow leaves backlit like a bursting roman candle. That is, when the sweat isn't stinging my eyes.

And perhaps you're thinking, "Wimp! It's a privilege to see these wonders. Why aren't you composing a haiku!" I can't help but ask: "Is it your head that's on fire? And where exactly are you while calling me a wimp? Likely sitting in a soft chair watching football and enjoying chips and ice-cold beer."

Damn it, so I'm not Ed Abbey. But credit me this - at least I'm honest. Did Abbey, Muir or Thoreau never have a bad day outdoors? Did they never cower, never fill with self-doubt, never liken the desert to Satan's bowling alley? Could they actually have enjoyed these biting gnats that are delighted to have me sharing their shade?

"Why does it matter?" you ask. It matters because there is more than heat, gnats and lack of water beating me up down here. My ego is hurting because my spirit isn't filled with the joy of nature and I'm wondering what's wrong with me. Perhaps it would help if, like a marathon runner, I could anticipate a group of bystanders cheering me as I step over the finish line. But late tonight when I arrive at the top, I'll be greeted by darkness and an empty truck. If the truck feels like me, the tires will be flat.

Ed, John, Henry, why not let me feel good even though I've had but a few brief moments of wonder during my eleven-hour ordeal? Issa, mentor-friend, it's your words, not theirs, that nurse my wounded spirit.

> listen, all you fleas,
> you can come on pilgrimage, okay,
> but then, off you get!
>
> ~ Issa, trans. D. Lanoue

Ruckus

If my birth date moves in its usual trajectory, it will come to mind occasionally today, perhaps due to a miscreant well-wisher, then briefly linger in the shadows, and finally pass on without raising much fuss.

Breakfast is a present to myself – a scone smothered in bittersweet Damson Plum jam and a cup of black Yunan tea.

While pretending to be unaffected, I do notice I've penned words that portend more ruckus than calm: "smothered," "miscreant well-wisher," "bittersweet," and "black" – all shadow moods associated with aging.

> late harvest –
> a plum bruised
> from the fall
>
> waning moon –
> rustle of leaves
> on the plum tree

Sunspot

Dr. Johnson takes a quick look at a small scab on my forehead, says "Sunspot, let's get it off." While he's busy putting tools on a tray, I manage to stammer, "Is that another word for skin cancer?"

"No, no," he says, leaning over so that he can get at it. "Here, just a bit of freezing."

Time seems frozen as he drops it into a plastic vial, sews me up and says. "Just a bit of skin, that. We'll send it to the lab and I'll want to see you next week to take the stitches out."

"And what's your guess?" I manage to say.

"Don't worry, it's good that you came right in. My best friend waited 6 months and it was too late. He died at 52."

On the drive home, his words flash through my mind: *tiny bit of skin, cancer, died at 52, waited too long, don't worry*. How long was it on my forehead before I noticed it?

Back home, I walk into the living room and say "Hi" to my daughter. She says "Hi dad" without looking up from her reading.

Everything seems just as I left it an hour ago. Yet everything seems different.

>   stretched out
>   in a sunspot –
>   the black and white cat

Talking About Things

The doorbell rings, and my wife greets Gayle and son, Brad. Gayle is petite and has a toothpaste ad smile. Brad is a gangly young teen, his eyes cast down.

I say "Hi" and continue working at the kitchen table. But I can't help overhearing their conversation.

"Brad has a new jacket. He likes blue. Don't you think he looks great!" says Gayle.

"Oh, yeah, very nice," my wife replies.

"He got it for the dance. He has a date with Jenny's daughter, Terri. She's cute as a button."

"I know her. I think she's an honors student," replies my wife.

"Brad, too. He wants to be a biologist."

Brad is examining the carpet as if he indeed loves biology and sees hundreds of interesting bugs crawling about on it.

"What about it, Brad," I say. "Is Biology your thing?"

"Oh, I donno," he says without looking up.

I kick myself. *Why did I keep him on the hot spot?*

Memories – my mother is telling Aunt Laura that I want to be a doctor, that the girls like me, that I got the best newspaper delivery award. Aunt Laura says, "Yes, he's such a good looking boy and pats my head." I do my best to become invisible, not easy when two Italian women are rolling your psyche back and forth like a bocce ball.

I entertain the idea of interjecting with, *Why don't we let Brad speak for himself*, but don't.

>   houseflies buzzing –
>   the sun shifted
>   behind a cloud

My Reader

She's in a meadow feeling a bit daring, making daisy chains, one to drape like a necklace to cover her sweet bosom and another to weave into silver-streaked curls.

She won't mind having reached this birthday. The day's been set aside to celebrate having gotten beyond the empty nest and her ex who's living with someone younger. It's time to dream of things she'll do from today on.

A picnic is spread on her Navajo blanket, bought in New Mexico. It brings to mind Ian Tyson's song about a romantic interlude with a lover on a blanket woven with a turtle dove pattern and streaks of lightening. Her basket holds a bottle of Pinot Noir, a loaf of farmer's 7-grain bread, an aged Gouda cheese (age is good!), and a macintosh apple.

She'll inhale the bouquet, sip, lay back, drift with clouds, soak in the sun's warmth and consider things absent from her life for far too long.

And now she's opened the book to one of my haibun, read it several times and says aloud, "Oh! I'd love to hear you read this."

> poetry reading –
> that silver-haired woman's
> radiant smile

Note: Modeled on Ted Kooser's poem, "Selecting a Reader," from *Sure Signs*, 1980, University of Pittsburgh Press, Pittsburgh, Pa.

Lost Canyon

Everything here slips toward the canyon's rim
- boulders, cobbles, pebbles, grains of sand -
and finally drops over into the Colorado. The
river's massive flow will continue to grind all
into silt and carry it into the Pacific Ocean.

I can't resist nudging a cobble. Seconds later,
there's a barely audible "plunk!"

Sitting side-by-side with my companion, our
feet dangling over the edge, I'm slipping
toward her, afraid to let go, afraid of the
free fall into the complexities of relationship
- lusting, bonding, loving, declaring -
afraid of those everythings we carry with us.

almost sunset -
our shadows mingle
on ancient stone

Section 2: Articles

Modern English Language Haibun

The term 'haibun' comes from the travel journal writing of the poet-monk Matsuo Basho who wrote in the 17th century and who is perhaps the most famous of the Japanese Master haiku poets. His classic travel journal, *The Narrow Road to the Deep North* (*Oku No Hosomichi*), was based on several months-long journeys through Japan. He called the work haibun which translates as "haiku writing" - narrative poetic prose interspersed with haiku.

English-language haibun emerged only in the late 1900s and was initially structured after the styles of Basho and other Japanese poets. But English-language haibun composition has evolved beyond the practice of Japanese masters to suit the needs of the English language and the tastes of contemporary readers. For example, most published contemporary haibun have subjects other than travel. They are of experiences related to the writer's friendship and family relationships, romantic life, retirement, aging and infirmity, philosophical musings, end-of-life experiences, fantasies and dreams.

Here are some characteristics of typical contemporary haibun that differentiate it from flash fiction, short stories and prose poetry:

1. Most haibun contains three basic elements: title, prose and haiku. Few short stories or flash fiction contain poetry, and ever fewer include haiku.

2. Haibun storylines tend to read as personal accounts and plausibly true. Short stories and flash fiction tend to read as fictional, that is, writing with made up characters and storylines. While it is commonly assumed that the short story and flash fiction storlines and characters are derived from the writer's experiences, haibun writing more clearly indicates that that the storyline is about the writer. However, some haibunists create fictional storylines that are written to sound as if they actually happened.

3. As with most writing genres like novels, short stories and flash fiction, haibun writers embellish their stories, exaggerating certain aspects, leaving out others and polishing the language in the service of providing good reading. The aim is to convey a sense of the events while providing enticing prose.

4. Many haibun tell the story as if it's happening now by employing first person, present tense. However, some haibun poets write pieces in the past tense or use a mix of past and present and some use second or third person.

5. Haibun fall roughly into two types. Narrative haibun has prose that focuses heavily on description with few if any poetic devices such as similes, metaphors, allusions, alliteration or repetition. Literary haibun prose tends to make more use of poetic flourishes and thus it more closely resembles prose poetry.

6. Most contemporary English-language haiku have two distinct phrases that work together to create a poetic spark and that display a moment of time in the poet's life. The haiku generally average about 13 syllables, just long enough to be said in one breath. This differs from an initial misunderstanding of Japanese haiku which have 17 Japanese-language sound units and which are not the same as English-language syllables. Few of today's published haiku follow a 5-7-5 pattern. Thus haiku has become a kind of free verse.

7. The haiku is typically different than, yet connected (linked) to the prose. It can add a new dimension to the storyline or serve to summarize a key feeling or sentiment.

8. Haiku typically use imagistic phrases different than those found in the prose phrases and that may or may not come from a setting described in the prose.

9. In general, the connection between haiku and prose is neither too obvious, nor too oblique.

10. Encountering the haiku causes a shift in the reader's mind from one kind of state (as in simply reading a story) to a different kind of state - getting a sense of the writer's haiku moment and thinking about its connection the story. It's akin to looking at a photo in an article and sensing its connection to the contents.

Note: Opinions vary at this stage of the development of English language haibun. Other editors and writers will naturally disagree with one or more of my pronouncments about haibun. So rather that treating these 10 items as commandments written in stone or thinking of the author as wooly-headed, it's best to consider them as written in putty, as food for thought. Surely each of us has broken one of the 10 Commandments without everlasting ill effect.

Writing Haibun: One Writer's Approach

From an Interview by Jeffrey Woodward, Editor, *Haibun Today*

Q: Ray, Your published haibun are numerous. An attempt to single out one as representative or characteristic would likely be misleading. Instead, I would prefer to ask you to refer to your haibun "Unsaddled" (pg. 16), one that I know well, and simply allow you to place it, for the reader, in its proper context.

An important aspect of my storytelling is an intent to express the fullness of the human psyche or as Jungian psychologists would put it, the shadow side, as well as the more open or socially acceptable side of the self. The haibun "Unsaddled" isn't an abstract essay on the pros and cons of retirement and reading the news, nor is it an optimistic piece about the joys of retirement. Instead it offers a glimpse of how one person experiences post-retirement mornings.

Most of my haibun are autobiographical. They 'out' the real me as best I know myself. Some contain observations and feelings that would not normally be discussed openly and that might be uncomfortable for others to read. There is a feel of 'confessional' to some of them.

This idea of 'outing' oneself is not very common if I judge by the haibun I read in the journals. Nor should it necessarily be. But I often get the impression that for some writers, life is but a walk in a garden amongst flowers, birds and butterflies, as if there are no predators in the wild or even in the garden.

Thus, "Unsaddled" is an attempt to expose the light and dark sides of retirement and reading the news as I experience them.

Related to this is that I'd like my haibun to offer the possibility of introspection to the reader. While a young person or a non-retiree reading "Unsaddled" might not identify with my experience, I think that most most people who are dismayed by what is presented in today's news and/or who are retired will recognize aspects of themselves in the piece even if they still watch and read the news.

Another aspect of my writing in "Unsaddled" is that I've connected my experience to that of writers from the past whom I admire and who might not otherwise be read by today's readers.

Q: The haibun "Trying It On" (pg. 77) and others you've had published contain dialogues. This was rather rare in much of the early writing in haibun. What prompts putting dialogues into haibun like the one below?

I select a dialogue as a subject for the same reason others might select an outstanding moment in nature or a significant aspect of a travel journey. Something in the conversation led to an emotional reaction (joy, irritation, confusion, sadness) about what transpired and I want to write about it.

Let me deconstruct "Trying It On" a bit. Paragraph 1 contains part of an external dialogue between myself and

a woman I had been dating for several months. As an aside, we're still good friends and we had a good discussion about my take on the her use of the word "comfortable."

Paragraph 2 switches to what I call an internal dialogue—my unspoken musings about her initial statement. These musings aren't precisely what went though my mind at the time. They're a polished embellishment, hopefully humorous, of my associations with the appellation "comfortable."

Paragraph 3 represents the external dialogue I had with her. It's an embellishment of what I replied and thought at the time and afterwards and is meant to provide a lightness by exaggerating my reaction.

And there's more to this piece. Japanese haiku masters like Issa who so often used humor have influenced my writing. I can't know whether readers will find humor in the piece, but I enjoyed letting my "macho" self have a full fling at being described as "comfortable." In similar vein, men I know flinch a bit at being described as 'nice'. Down deep, I think many of us guys want to be seen as exciting, not just nice or comfy and perhaps even daredevilish or even dangerous. I think this comes from my high-school experiences where I watched the (I want to say "dumb") jocks and bad boys got the gals I was attracted to.

Both haiku are desk-ku, that is made up. Some would call them senryu. I rode a motorcycle when I was younger and often have the urge to buy a Harley—not the Hell's Angels type, but more the road-trip bike. This isn't so far from the truth in that when I was a whitewater kayaker, I drove around town displaying my kayak on top of my truck. This male "look-at-me" trip went on even when it was snowing outside. As far as the second haiku goes, a catalogue didn't arrive in the mail, but a friend, weary of hearing me express my mock desire for a bike, gave me a Harley catalogue. Nor did I cruise a tattoo parlor three times or even once. The haiku was meant to be a humorous depiction of a man who is, in fact, ambivalent about getting a tattoo, but who *kinda* wants one. That's me. And no, I don't have a cobra tattoo etched on my big toenail or anywhere else.

Q: You published your first haibun in early 2000. What has changed in your writing, in terms of style or content, over that period?

Previous to writing haiku and haibun, I wrote essays and, of course, articles throughout my career as an academic social scientist. So the important transformation was from writing longish and rather boorish didactic essays to writing concrete, experience-based micro-stories in the style of haibun.

But perhaps the biggest change has to do with subject matter as opposed to style. Over the last eight years, my writing has shifted from describing my experiences in exploring wilderness areas to a variety of themes including:

- retirement and aging.
- fall romance—the world of romance for those of us who are past middle age.
- family issues including marriage, divorce and raising children in the era of drugs, sex and the new media.
- memoirs of childhood, school and parents.
- loss—the death of parents, friends, spouses, children and even animal companions.

Related to this, I've begun to focus on putting together themed collections mixing photography, haibun, haiku and tanka poetry.

Q: How and when, Ray, were you first drawn to haibun?

In the late 1980s I took up photography and linked that to an interest in webpage design. I created a website focused on my images of the Kurimoto Japanese Garden near my home. I wanted to add Asian poetry to the website, searched the Internet and discovered that strange little beast called haiku. It struck me that haiku composition is akin to photography. Landscape photographers find elements in the chaos of nature that catch the eye and make them stand out visually. Haiku poets do much the same with words.

I next began creating websites that combined digital art and photographs with the haiku of contemporary poets and the Japanese Masters. Through this, I developed a deeper feeling for haiku and began to write my own.

My excursion into haibun began several years later. I wanted to write about certain events in my personal life to share with family and friends. The haiku form felt too small a snapshot for that aim, and haibun, with its prose component and focus on the personal, struck me as a suitable vehicle. British poet and humorist Roger McGough expressed my need for a more expansive form than haiku with this little haiku-like ditty:

> the only problem
> with haiku is that you just
> get started and then

Haibun allows you to get it said, albeit in a distinctly succinct prose style, and offers the challenge of linking a haiku to the prose in a way that enchances both.

Q: Several years ago, you joined the staff of *Haibun Today*, and you've been a haibun editor for three other journals prior to that. Has this new role altered your perspective on the haibun community? Or has it confirmed your prior opinions?

I'd been reluctant to serve as an editor, in part because it's a lot of work to conscientiously read submissions and make a decision, and in part because I hate to say *"no"* to any writer who is giving haibun a try. I'm also aware of my biases in haibun composition and feel awkward being a judge of another person's work.

In the end, I said "*yes*" when invited to edit because I thought haibun journals are important and someone has to volunteer. I also felt that I should serve the haiku community given that the work of other volunteer editors allowed me to find places for my writing to be published.

The work submitted to journals that I edit often leads me to think that if only haibunists were members of a writing workshop, their pieces could be enhanced through candid feedback from other writers and the resultant revision process. But there aren't many opportunities for detailed feedback prior to submission for publication. So that leaves the task to the editors.

Many editors don't provide feedback because there is sometimes an adverse response from a writer. But I've been grateful that some do and have benefited from their advice.

I provide feedback as part of my editing practice. This makes editing a lot more work than simply saying "yes" or "no." And while I've had some negative or defensive reactions, almost all positive.

A danger is that a writer will feel bound to accept an editor's suggestions as a means of getting his or her work published. I know that I do when an editor makes a suggestion about my work. A further danger is that an editor's feedback creates an implicit demand for revisions fitting the editor's style. Thus, without meaning to, editors may create a pressure on writers to copy the editors' voices and styles.

Q: What role do you foresee for short form poetry journals in the future growth of haibun?

I think that the present mix of print and online journals publishing haibun is about right—that is, dedicated writers now have numerous venues in which to get their work published, particularly if they're willing to accept feedback and the ups and downs of rejection or, as writer-colleague Neal Whitman put it, if they're willing to put up with an editor's "subjection."

Growth is also indicated by the number of new writers working in the genre. They come from haiku, from free verse and prose poetry and from flash fiction and personal journal practices.

A reasonable maturity in writing haibun comes after 5 or 10 years. So the prospects are good that we'll have a polished new cadre of writers appearing in future issues and that the overall quality of writing will continue to improve.

While the genre doesn't need new journals at this point, writering forums are needed that provide candid feedback processes and there's a need for more literary criticism on published work in order to help new writers develop their skills and volunteer editors to better understand their genre. That is, reading literary criticism should make volunteer editors both more demanding and yet more open to stylistic variations in haibun composition.

Q: How would you compare the haibun scene of today to that of five or seven years ago? What are the prospects for haibun tomorrow?

I like to think that the popularity of haibun—both the reading and writing of the form—will continue to grow. There's been a parallel growth of the similar forms like flash fiction. In part, that's because haibun and flash fiction are forms of storytelling and it's easy for the general reader to relate to a well-told story

Billy Collins, a past poet laureate of the U.S., has produced a best-selling collection of poems selected for being reader-friendly. His premise is that poetry readership will increase when there is less obliqueness in the genre and poets quit writing exclusively for other poets and begin writing for the general public. This is not to say that there's not a place for more complex, allusion-oriented (oblique) poetry. It's that the subjects and styles used in haibun tend to be more reader-friendly than, for example, free verse and prose poetry.

As a final point, we seem to be entering an era of watching as opposed to reading and writing. Others have commented on the dumbing down of writing through social media like twitter where polished, comprehensive, thoughtful writing isn't happening. People once made their own music in social settings; now music is made for them to consume. This isn't to say that today's music is lacking; just that there's been a loss in that so many fewer of us are making our own music.

Note: This is an Abridged version of an interview originally published in *Haibun Today* 5:1 March 2011.

Haibun Resources

Haibun (and its close cousin, tanka prose) can be read online through a variety of journals including these three:

- http://haibuntoday.com
- http://contemporaryhaibunonline.com
- http://ahundredgourds.com

The print journals *Bottle Rockets*, *Blithe Spirit*, *Frogpond* and *Modern Haiku* carry haiku and haibun.

A full listing of haibun and haiku journals can be found on the "Haiku Genre Journals Online & Print" website: http://raysweb.net/haikujournals/

The website "Haibun & Tanka Prose Resources" contains a collection of online and print resources about haibun and tanka prose: http://raysweb.net/haibunresources/

The website "Haiku, Haibun, Haiga" contains articles, commentaries, reviews and interviews by the author: http://raysweb.net/haiku/pages/articles.html

Three themed websites by the author are:

- Canyonlands Journal:
  http://raysweb.net/canyonlandsjournal
- Romance under a Waning Moon:
  http://raysweb.net/fallromance
- Day's End: Poetry and Photography about Aging:
  http://raysweb.net/daysend

Section 3:

Biography & Acknowledgments

About the Author

Ray Rasmussen lives at times in Edmonton, Alberta, Canada and at times in Halton Hills, Ontario, Canada. He has been composing haibun since the late 90s. His work appears regularly in a many of the international journals that carry haibun. A number of his haibun are included in the anthologies, *Contemporary Haibun*, *Journeys 2014*, the *Red Moon Anthology* and the British Haiku Society's anthologies, *The Unseen Wind* and *Dover Beach and My Back Yard*. Currently, he serves as haibun editor for the online journal *Haibun Today*.

When he's not busy writing and editing, he spends a good deal of his time hiking, canoeing and photographing wilderness places, including Alberta's Willmore Wilderness and Jasper National Parks, Utah's Canyonlands National Park and Ontario's Algonquin Provincial Park.

In a previous life, Ray was a professor and chair of the Department of Strategic Management and Organization, the TransAlta Professor of Environmental Policy, and the Director of the Environmental Research and Studies Centre at the University of Alberta in Edmonton.

Ray provides online coaching for writers in haibun composition. He can be reached at ray@raysweb.net

Acknowledgments

Throughout my writing career, I've been given great help and encouragement by Jeffrey Woodward, colleague and Editor of *Haibun Today*; by my partner, Nancy Hull, and friends Gary Ford and Kathy Caine; by my friend, Florence Ross who provided the tools through which I produced this book; by various "hands on" journal editors who are willing to take the time to make suggestions about individual submissions; by Glenn Coats, my co-editor at *Haibun Today*; by poet Angelee Deodhar, editor of *Journeys* 2014 & 2015; by the members of the Haibun Writers Workshop; and by writer-poet Jim Dodds as a copy editor, content and formatting advisor.

My thanks to the editors of the following periodicals for first publishing the haibun and articles reprinted herein: *A Hundred Gourds, Bottle Rockets, Blithe Spirit, Contemporary Haibun Online, Frogpond, Haibun Today, Lynx, Modern Haiku, Modern Haibun and Tanka Prose, Multiverses, Notes from the Gean, Simply Haiku*, and the British Haiku Society's haibun contest anthologies: *Dover Beach and My Backyard*, 2007 and *The Unseen Wind*, 2009.

It's difficult for a writer to reread previously published haibun and not tinker with them, even though they've been accepted and published. I've yielded to the 'endless revision' impulse and many of the pieces have been tinkered with. But none are far from the originals as they appeared in publications.

Section 4: Haibun Index

Colophon: Inuksuk Landmarks

The title of this book has to do with the author's fixation on the mysterious and evocative stone figures known as *inuksuit* (plural of *inuksuk*) – lardmarks that are found throughout the vast Artic landscape. Some resemble a human form while others are a seemingly random pile of stones.

Built by Inuit peoples from whatever stones are at hand, each *inuksuk* is a uniquely shaped, nuanced form of communication in a somewhat featureless terrain. They serve as navigational aids, offer information about places to hunt and fish, and indicate caches of food, supplies and camps. Some may have signaled places of veneration or the abodes of spirit beings.

Importantly, some are a kind of artwork, made while passing the time while waiting for tides or weather conditions to permit travel to a next destination. These are called *inuksuapik*, built with the greatest of care, their shape as well as the colour and texture of the stones making them stand out from the other types.

And many are simply remnants – scatters of stones that once signaled something.

remnants –
memories scattered over
a hundred pages

Information from Norman Hallendy, *Inuksuit: Silent Messingers of the Arctic,* Douglas & McIntyre, Vancouver/Toronto, First Paperback Edition, 2001 and the Wikipedia website "Inuit".

Landmarks

A Haibun Collection
Ray Rasmussen

Translation of Inuksuk

~Someone was here ~

Haibun Bookshelf Publishing

Edmonton, Canada 2015

http://raysweb.net/hbp

Proof

Made in the USA
Charleston, SC
25 August 2015